ISBN 978-1-5278-2726-4
PIBN 10893225

Historic, archived document

Do not assume content reflects current
scientific knowledge, policies, or practices.

Mothers' Opinions of

FIBERS IN CHILDREN'S CLOTHES

UNITED STATES DEPARTMENT OF AGRICULTURE
AGRICULTURAL MARKETING SERVICE
MARKET DEVELOPMENT RESEARCH DIVISION

PREFACE

With the entrance of new synthetic fibers and blends into
the apparel field, information about consumers' reactions
to the various materials available becomes increasingly
important to those concerned with the production and marketing of cotton and wool. This report deals with mothers'
attitudes toward agriculturally produced fibers and their
competitors in various clothing items worn by children 1
through 13 years of age. It is one of a number of studies
on farm products and their end uses conducted by the Market
Development Research Division, and is part of a broad pro-
gram of research aimed at improving marketing efficiency
and expanding markets for farm products.

This study, an extension of earlier work in this field,
should prove of interest and use to producer groups, to
manufacturers of children's clothing, to textile mills,
and to researchers engaged in developing fiber products
more acceptable to the consumer. Much of the data can
also serve industry as background for promotional and edu-
cational programs aimed at increasing the market for agricultural fibers.

The project was under the general direction of Trienah
Meyers. Consultation and technical advice were provided
during the planning stage by the National Cotton Council
of America; The Wool Bureau, Inc.; E. I. duPont deNemours
and Co.; American Cotton Manufacturers Institute, Inc.;
Deering, Milliken and Co., Inc.; and the Celanese Corporation of America.

Opinion Research Corporation, of Princeton, N. J., de-
veloped the questionnaire, conducted the survey, and pre-
pared a draft of the report under contract with the United
States Department of Agriculture.

September 1960

C O N T E N T S

H I G H L I G H T S

Fiber Preferred for Seven Clothing Items

Cotton was regarded as the outstanding fiber for children's clothing, according to the opinions expressed by a representative sample of 2,476 mothers who were interviewed in a nationwide study. It was the leading fiber for the first six of the clothing items shown in the tabulation below; wool was the preferred fiber for the seventh. Among the manmade fibers, nylon was generally the leader. It was almost in equal favor with cotton for girls' dress-up dresses and a strong second choice as the best material for slips. Listed below are the materials preferred by 10 percent or more of the mothers for each of these items of clothing:

Item 1/	Material preferred by 10 percent or more of the mothers interviewed		
	Cotton	Nylon	Wool
	Percent	Percent	Percent
Schoolboys' sport shirts --------	78	--	--
Boys' pants for school wear -----	87		
Schoolgirls' blouses ------------	71		
Schoolgirls' dress-up dresses ---	38	33	
Schoolgirls' slips --------------	62	28	
Girls' skirts for school wear ---	41		26
Outer jackets or short coats ----	22	--	34

Cotton has many virtues in the minds of those mothers who preferred it for the various items of clothing. Most comments centered around cotton's ease of care and other laundering properties, its nice appearance, and its durable wearing qualities. Corduroy was thought to have the additional advantage of warmth.   The need for ironing and difficulties with ironing were the disadvantages mentioned most often by the few mothers who had anything unfavorable to say about cotton.

Wool was considered desirable as a skirt and outer jacket material mainly because of its warmth, good appearance, and durability.

1/ Each of these clothing items was owned by all or almost all of the girls or boys.

Nylon, preferred by many mothers for dress-up dresses and slips, was praised mainly for laundering qualities, particularly its minimal ironing requirements, and its attractiveness. As a dress material, nylon was criticized primarily for not being cool and for fraying and raveling at the seams. Its principal disadvantages as a slip material, according to mothers, is its tendency to turn grey or dingy, and its warmth.

Material Preferred for Rainwear

Three-fifths of the mothers of school children reported their sons and daughters had raincoats. Plastic, treated cotton, and rubber-coated cotton ranked almost equally as preferred materials for girls' rainwear. The materials mothers preferred for boys' raincoats were rubber-coated cotton, oilskin, and plastic, in that order.

Rubber-coated cotton and oilskin were liked primarily because of their water-repellent and durability qualities. Plastic's major appeals lie in its waterproofness, lower price, light weight, easy cleaning, and convenience of carrying. Treated cotton coats are considered attractive, durable, and suitable for many occasions.

"No need for them" was the usual explanation given for children not wearing raincoats, often because door-to-door transportation was provided between home and school on rainy days. About 1 in 4 felt they could not afford raincoats, and some children, especially school-age boys, disliked wearing them.

Anklets and Socks

Stretch socks are a popular type of footwear for children under 14. About 9 out of 10 mothers reported that their children had worn them. Mothers divided about evenly in the preference for stretch or regular socks.

In discussing the good points of stretch socks, those who preferred them emphasized comfort and fit factors (fit smoothly, don't need to worry about size, etc.), and durability. Mothers who liked regular socks better cited a variety of reasons for their choice: Not turning grey or dingy, durability, and absorbency were mentioned a little more often than other considerations.

"Wash-and-Wear"

Three-fourths of all mothers covered in the survey reported that their children had worn "wash-and-wear" garments. They praised the easy-care features of this type of clothing; the 4 users in 10 who had some criticism spoke mainly of the necessity for some ironing. When asked to cite a preference among the various materials, about 4 in 10 said it didn't make any difference to them, 28 percent voted for all cotton, 17 percent chose manmade fibers, and 16 percent liked "wash-and-wear" items made of a mixture of the two.

54 percent) of the mothers interviewed indicated
.dren's woolen clothing items in the past year or so,
ie mother in five who had washed wool expressed dis-
;ults, shrinkage being the major complaint.

l and Disposed of

:nts covered in this survey were purchased new by
is within the family or from friends and relatives
; were also mentioned frequently. Home sewing was
.tems, particularly dresses and skirts.

iothers indicated that they usually give outgrown
:latives; most of the remainder hand them down within
ray for future use.

ng Selection

;, children take considerable interest in the kinds
exert quite a bit of influence on their selection.
·ls display considerably more interest in clothing
older children are more interested than younger ones.

·ol children 6 to 13 were asked where their children
; of clothes to wear the typical reply was "from other
 Relatively few mothers reported such sources of
iagazines. In the case of pre-schoolers, family mem-
·lder brothers or sisters -- are important sources of

This publication contains a summarization of major findings; it is not a comprehensive presentation of all the data collected in the study. Those interested in the complete tabulations (including crossbreaks by variables such as family income), the sample design, and the questionnaire used, are referred to a separate volume titled SUPPLEMENT TO: "MOTHERS' OPINIONS OF FIBERS IN CHILDREN'S CLOTHES." Anyone desiring a free copy of the Supplement should address his request to:

Market Development Research Division
Agricultural Marketing Service
U. S. Department of Agriculture
Washington 25, D. C.

MOTHERS' OPINIONS OF FIBERS

IN CHILDREN'S CLOTHES

by Margaret Weidenhamer, project director
Market Development Research Division
Agricultural Marketing Service

INTRODUCTION

Scope and Organization of the Report

were interviewed on such topics as their experience with var-
predominant material currently in use, preference and reasons
and either disadvantages of the preferred material or ratings
rs on selected attributes (for example, ease of care and dura-
following items of children's clothes:

Outer jackets or short coats
Anklets and socks (stretch vs. "regular")
Schoolgirls' slips and dress-up dresses
Girls' blouses and skirts for school wear
Schoolgirls' rainwear
Schoolboys' rainwear
Schoolboys' sport shirts
Boys' pants for school wear

re also questioned briefly about what children usually wear in
lr clothing is obtained and disposed of, children's interest in
1 the clothing they wear, and mothers' experience with children's
clothes, and washing wool clothes.

:ation discusses the major findings, and presents some of the
or chart form. A Supplement to this report, which is available
tains the detailed tables, description of the sample and inter-
res, and a copy of the questionnaire.

When and with Whom Interviews were Taken

1g was conducted during June and July 1958. The findings re-
based on 2,476 personal interviews conducted among a probability
rs with children 1 through 13 years of age living in private
1e United States. (A detailed discussion of the sample appears
1t to this report.)

Cautions in Interpreting the Data

Every survey in which interviews are conducted with less than 100 percent of the people whose opinions are being studied is subject to some possible sampling variation. For the results of this study, approximate confidence limits for various survey percentages have been calculated by standard statistical techniques and are shown in the Supplement.

Any survey data are also subject, to some degree, to response error; inadvertent misstatements by respondents may occur because of lack of information or oversight. It is especially important to keep this in mind when analyzing data on fiber experience, since faulty recall and difficulties with fiber identification undoubtedly have some influence on the validity of respondents' statements about what materials they have used.

Response error stemming from misconceptions of the fiber content of certain garments would be a major concern if the data were intended to provide estimates of fiber consumption. Since the interest in this study was the relationship among experience, preference, and opinions about various materials, even respondents' impressions about what they have used are valuable. However, it was considered important to minimize errors which could result from respondents forgetting to mention some of the materials they had used, or confusing various fiber or trade names. In an effort to counter these problems, interviewers read the following introductory statement to respondents before any questions about fiber experience were asked:

> As you know, children's clothes are made from many materials these days. By materials, we mean fibers like nylon or cotton, and also blends of two or three fibers such as cotton and Dacron mixed, or wool, nylon and rayon mixed, etc. There are so many materials nowadays that we made up this card (HAND RESPONDENT CARD A) to help you recall what various items of your children's clothes are made of. This list isn't complete, since new fibers and blends are being introduced every day, so if any of the garments that we will be discussing are made from other materials, just tell me so.

Card A, which the respondent was asked to refer to throughout the course of the interview, listed the more usual fibers and mixtures that are found in children's clothing items. Although rayon and acetate were listed separately on the card, they were later combined because many women do not distinguish between these two fibers. (See Supplement for actual contents of Card A and additional information about the questionnaire.)

CHILDREN'S USE OF AND ATTITUDES TOWARD CLOTHING

Interest in and Influence on Clothes Worn

ey data indicate that, in the opinion of their mothers, many
considerable interest in the kinds of clothes they wear and exert
f influence on their selection.

ee of concern children evidence depends to a large extent on both
with sex being the more crucial factor. As shown in the tabula-
irls display considerably more interest in clothing selection than
er children are more interested than younger ones. The proportion
o described their children as being "very interested" in clothing
ged from 73 percent of the mothers of school-age girls (6 to 13
percent of the mothers of pre-school boys (3 to 5 years).

ld you say your ____ year old (boy, girl) is very interested,
ly interested, or not very interested in what kinds of clothes
get (or make) for (him, her)?"

	Girls 6 to 13	Girls 3 to 5	Boys 6 to 13	Boys 3 to 5
	Percent	Percent	Percent	Percent
interested -----	73	51	43	27
ly interested ---	18	25	35	33
very interested -	9	24	22	40
	(T-66)	(T-21)	(T-33)	(T-10)

: Complete tabulations of the above findings, showing detailed results for community size, family income, and
   other characteristics studied are presented in the
   Supplement to this report. Throughout this report, the
   T- references are to the detailed tables in the Supplement.

age are also important factors in how much "say" children have
ds of clothes selected for them. In this respect, however, age
ortant factor than sex.   Note in the following tabulation that
 girls 6 to 13 have, according to mothers, considerably more "say"
g selection than boys or girls 3 to 5.

"All in all, how much say does (he, she) have in what kinds of clothes you get (or make) for (him, her) -- quite a bit, only a little, or practically no say?"

	Girls 6 to 13 Percent	Boys 6 to 13 Percent	Girls 3 to 5 Percent	Boys 3 to 5 Percent
Quite a bit ---------	58	43	26	20
Only a little -------	29	34	30	22
Practically none ----	13	23	44	58
	(T-68)	(T-35)	(T-23)	(T-12)

Sources of Ideas

Girls 6 to 13 years

According to mothers, school-age girls get their ideas about clothing primarily from other girls their own age. By comparison, all other sources are minor. Here are the ones that mothers mentioned most often: Other girls their age (62 percent); mothers (14 percent); older girls (12 percent); television (12 percent); sisters (10 percent); and magazines (10 percent). (T-67)

There are variations in the above pattern depending on the girl's exact age. Magazines are consulted somewhat more often by girls 12 and over than by younger girls. Mothers are consulted less frequently for ideas by girls over 10 than those under 10. (T-67)

Girls 3 to 5 years

Pre-school girls get most of their ideas about clothing from their mothers, sisters, and other girls their age. The major influences reported by mothers of girls in this age group are: Mothers (29 percent); other girls their age (21 percent); sisters (20 percent); television (15 percent); and older girls (10 percent). (T-22)

Boys 6 to 13 years

The pattern of idea sources on clothing for school-age boys is similar to that reported for school-age girls. Boys in this age group look primarily to boys their own age for clothing ideas. The main sources reported by mothers are: Other boys their age (60 percent); fathers (14 percent); and older boys (12 percent). (T-34)

Boys 3 to 5 years

Boy friends, fathers, and older brothers are mentioned about equally often as the origin of clothing ideas for boys under 6. Here are the principal idea sources that mothers report for this age group: Other boys their age (23 percent); fathers (22 percent); brothers (20 percent); and older boys (12 percent). (T-11)

Play Clothes Worn

Mothers were asked to indicate from a list of selected items the ones their children usually wear for play during the winter. Similar questions were asked about the kinds of clothes that are usually worn for dress occasions and for school. Most of the respondents were able to specify the types of garments worn most frequently, but some mothers indicated that their children wore different types of garments equally often for certain occasions.

Boys 1 to 5 years

Knitted shirts and dungarees are the items worn most often by boys under 6 for winter play. Knitted shirts are mentioned by 80 percent of the mothers, and dungarees by 63 percent. For outdoor play, jackets (41 percent) and snowsuits (42 percent) are the most common outer garments. The reported use of these items varies somewhat by age. According to mothers' testimony, usage of sport shirts, dungarees, and outer jackets is more common among boys 3 - 5. (T-6)

Boys 6 to 13 years

The garments worn most often for play during the winter by boys in this age group are dungarees, knitted shirts, and outer jackets. Dungarees are cited by 92 percent of the mothers, knitted shirts by 60 percent, and outer jackets by 67 percent. (T-30)

Girls 1 to 5 years

Girls under 6 wear about the same kinds of clothes for winter play as boys in the same age group. Knitted shirts are mentioned by 77 percent of the mothers, dungarees by 48 percent, and slacks by 33 percent. Snowsuits (42 percent) led outer jackets (28 percent) for outdoor play. (T-17)

Girls 6 to 13 years

Sweaters (47 percent), outer jackets (46 percent), knitted shirts (46 percent), and blouses (32 percent), along with dungarees (53 percent) and slacks (40 percent) are the principal items worn for winter play by schoolgirls. The use of these items varies sharply by age. There is a decrease in the use of knitted shirts and a corresponding increase in the use of blouses as girls approach 13. Use of slacks also increases with age. (T-62)

Dress Clothes Worn

Boys 1 to 5 years

Long pants, cited by 78 percent of the mothers, are favored for dress wear. In the shirt category, dress shirts (43 percent) were worn more often than sport shirts (36 percent) and knitted shirts (22 percent). Sport coats were mentioned by 28 percent; only 3 percent of the mothers report frequent use of two-piece suits. (T-7)

Boys 6 to 13 years

Long pants, dress shirts, sport coats and outer jackets are the items worn most often for dress by boys in this age group. Ninety percent of mothers mention long pants, 69 percent dress shirts, 53 percent sport coats, and 54 percent outer jackets in this connection. (T-29)

Girls 1 to 5 years

Girls under 6 use one-piece dresses almost exclusively for dress-up wear but are divided on outdoor garments. Ninety-two percent of the mothers say their girls usually wear a one-piece dress for such an occasion. Sweaters are mentioned by 41 percent, snowsuits by 30 percent, jackets by 25 percent, and coats by 21 percent. (T-18)

Girls 6 to 13 years

Like pre-school girls, girls of school age usually wear one-piece dresses for special occasions. This type of garment is reported by 81 percent of the mothers. Others reported as usually worn for dress are skirts (33 percent) and blouses (24 percent). Sweaters are cited by 36 percent; outer jackets (38 percent) or coats (32 percent) complete the outfit. Use of separates increases with age. For example, skirts are reported by 26 percent of the mothers of girls 6 to 7 years old and 43 percent of the mothers of girls 12 to 13. For blouses the percentages range from 19 percent to 29 percent. (T-62)

School Clothes Worn

Boys 6 to 13 years

Sport shirts and dungarees are the leaders for school wear during the winter. Mothers of boys 6 to 13 mentioned sport shirts (69 percent) and dungarees (64 percent) most often. Long pants (38 percent), sweaters (34 percent), and knitted shirts (31 percent) are less popular. Use of outer jackets is practically universal (83 percent). (T-28)

Girls 6 to 13 years

Skirts worn with either sweaters or blouses are favored for school wear. One-piece dresses are also popular. The principal garments discussed by mothers are: Skirts (66 percent), sweaters (68 percent), blouses (57 percent), and dresses (48 percent). Jackets (59 percent) are the leading item for outdoor wear. Use of skirts and blouses increases and use of dresses decreases as girls approach 13. (T-61)

Clothing Likes and Dislikes

To ascertain the popularity of various clothing items, mothers were asked to indicate, first, the ones their children particularly liked to wear, and second, the ones they didn't like to wear.

Girls appear to be more likely to have favorites than boys, and schoolage children more likely to than the younger ones.

One-piece dresses are the only item named frequently as favorites by mothers of pre-school girls. Those with daughters 6-13 cited dresses frequently, too, but skirts, blouses, and sweaters are also quite popular, especially with girls toward the upper end of this age bracket.

Items girls particularly like to wear

	Girls 6 to 13	Girls 1 to 5
	Percent	Percent
Skirts ----------------------	35	7
Dresses ---------------------	33	44
Blouses ---------------------	26	6
Sweaters --------------------	21	7
No particular item ---------	11	32
	(T-64)	(T-19)
	(Partial tabulations)	

Boys' main favorites are dungarees, but sport shirts, knitted shirts, long pants, and outer jackets also rated fairly high.

Items boys particularly like to wear

	Boys 6 to 13	Boys 1 to 5
	Percent	Percent
Dungarees -------------------	56	24
Sport shirts ---------------	26	9
Knitted shirts -------------	21	17
Long pants -----------------	15	13
Outer jackets --------------	15	7
No particular item ---------	19	47
	(T-31)	(T-8)
	(Partial tabulations)	

Children 6 and over are also somewhat more critical of certain items of clothing than are children under 6. Specific items "disliked" were named by 56 percent of mothers of boys 6 to 13, 42 percent of mothers of girls 6 to 13, 29 percent of mothers of boys 1 to 5, and 29 percent of mothers of girls 1 to 5.

Here are the principal items that mothers said their children didn't like to wear:

	6 to 13 years Percent	1 to 5 years Percent
Boys:		
Short pants ----------	23	9
Dress shirts ---------	19	6
Girls:		
Dungarees ------------	11	8
Dresses -------------	10	4
	(T-32, 65)	(T-9, 20)
	(Partial tabulations)	

How Clothing was Obtained

Most of the items of both girls' and boys' clothing asked about were purchased new by parents. However, hand-me-downs from older children in the family or the children of friends and relatives were mentioned frequently, and gifts of new clothing were also prevalent. Sport shirts and dress-up dresses were particularly popular as gift items; pre-school children were more likely to have received gifts of clothing than were those of school age. In addition, many of the girls in both age groups wore home-sewn dresses and skirts. (T-13-15, 24-26, 36-38, 69-71)

(NOTE: Sources of clothes for school-age boys and girls are discussed more fully under the headings of the specific garments.)

Disposing of Outgrown Clothing

There is considerable unanimity among mothers of boys and girls in both age groups on methods of disposing of outgrown clothes. Almost half indicated that they usually give such garments to friends or relatives; over 3 in 10 usually use them as hand-me-downs within the family or save them for the future A few give them to charities, and about 1 in 10 indicated that their children are hard enough on clothes that outgrown items are no longer suitable for wear.

"What do you do with most of (his, her) clothing that is still suitable for wear, but has been outgrown?"

	Boys 1 to 5 Percent	Boys 6 to 13 Percent	Girls 1 to 5 Percent	Girls 6 to 13 Percent
Give to friends or relatives ----	47	43	50	53
Give to or save for siblings ----	30	31	26	30
Give to charity -----------------	6	10	8	11
Save for possible future need ---	6	--	7	--
Other ---------------------------	3	3	3	2
It's usually worn out -----------	11	15	8	8
	(T-16)	(T-39)	(T-27)	(T-72)

MOTHERS' ATTITUDES TOWARD FIBERS IN SCHOOLBOYS' CLOTHING

The following is a detailed discussion of the competitive position of natural and manmade fibers in sport shirts, school pants, and raincoats worn by boys in the 6 to 13 age group. All but 1 percent of the mothers questioned reported their sons wore sport shirts; 57 percent indicated their boys wore raincoats. The survey data relate to mothers' use of and attitudes toward the fibers found in these three items of boys' clothing.

Sport Shirts

To insure that the term "sport shirt" had the same meaning for all respondents, interviewers were instructed to read the following definition before asking any questions about this type of shirt:

> Now, I'd like to talk about boys' sport shirts with either long or short sleeves -- the kinds that have a collar and button down the front. We are not interested in the knitted ones like polo shirts, T-shirts, or other pullovers.

Use of sport shirts

Sport shirts are widely used by boys in the 6 to 13 age bracket. More than 8 in 10 women reported that their sons had worn this type of shirt for school, play, and dress during the 12 months preceding the interview. (T-40)

Sources of sport shirts

New purchases were the major source of sport shirts for boys 6 to 13. Seven in 10 mothers said they bought most of their sons' sport shirts. "Hand downs" from older brothers, friends or relatives ranked next; they were reported as the most frequent source by about 15 percent of mothers. New gifts and home-sewn shirts were major sources for 9 percent and 5 percent of mothers, respectively. The additional sources mentioned most frequently were gifts (30 percent) and hand-me-downs (26 percent). (T-36)

Fiber experience and preference

As of 1958, when the survey was conducted, boys' sport shirts of synthetic fibers or mixtures had made little impact on the market. In this item of apparel, cotton maintained a commanding position, as shown in the tabulation below. Large majorities of women reported use of and preference for all-cotton sport shirts. Among the other fibers and mixtures reported, the Dacron and cotton combination was the most popular, in terms of current use and preference. Nylon had been tried by about 4 mothers in 10, but very few were using much of it currently or preferred it for boys' sport shirts.

Mothers' Reported Use of and Preference
for Selected Sport Shirt Fabrics

	Have used	Most shirts now worn are	Like best
	Percent	Percent	Percent
Cotton ---------------	96	90	78
Nylon ---------------	39	2	2
Rayon-cotton ---------	14	2	2
Rayon/acetate --------	13	1/	1/
Dacron-cotton --------	12	4	8
	(T-45)	(T-44)	(T-41)
		(Partial tabulations)	

1/ Too few cases to be shown separately.

Almost all of those who preferred cotton said it was the material most of their boys' sport shirts were made of; among those who preferred Dacron-cotton, 37 percent indicated it was the material they were using the most of at present, and 57 percent had tried it at some time for boys' sport shirts. (T-44, 45)

Satisfactions with preferred fiber

Cotton sport shirts.--Ease of care and launderability top a long list of factors women who preferred cotton for sport shirts discussed when asked what they liked best about it; they said such things as: Cotton is easy to iron, easy to wash, is machine-washable and irons well. Appearance and style factors were mentioned by 6 in 10, 3 in 10 mentioned durability, and about one in five cited comfort factors. (T-42)

Dacron-cotton sport shirts.--Ease of care, particularly as it relates to ironing, was the major appeal of Dacron-cotton sport shirts. Nine in 10 women who preferred this type of fabric for boys' sport shirts cited ease of care factors with slightly over half (51 percent) mentioning its minimum ironing requirements. Other factors cited were appearance (49 percent), durability (22 percent), and comfort (10 percent). (T-42)

Numbers preferring other materials were too small for separate analysis.

Dissatisfactions with preferred fiber

Very few women criticized either all-cotton or Dacron-cotton sport shirts. Eighty-five percent of the advocates of each type of sport shirt material reported nothing they disliked about their preferred fabric. The 15 percent who were critical cited these factors most often:

	Mothers who prefer --	
	Cotton	Dacron-cotton
	Percent	Percent
ing ---------	4	--
ance -------	3	3
iron --------	2	--
-----------	2	--
vell --------	2	3
-----------	1/ *	2

(T-43)

(Partial tabulations)

in 1 percent.

Boys' School Pants

ated that most of their boys' school pants were
of the mothers reported hand-me-downs as a major

ence for winter

of all other fabrics used in boys' pants. Almost
1 that their sons had worn regular-weave all-cotton
reported the use of corduroy. These were also the
at wardrobes and in preference for winter wear.
ys' pants was reported by almost half of the mothers,
1 it was the major fiber in current use or was their
school pants were negligible. (See explanation of
Interpreting Data," last paragraph.) About 1 in 5
l; it was reported as the predominant fiber in use
rred by the same proportion. Various wool blends
wool-nylon, wool-rayon, or wool-Orlon) had been
ne of these blends was mentioned by many mothers as
rrent use or as their preference.

Mothers' Reported Use of and Preference for Selected Fibers in Boys' School Pants

	Have used	Most pants worn are	Like best
	Percent	Percent	Percent
"Other" cotton ----------	96	76	57
Corduroy ----------------	82	20	30
Wool blends -------------	1/67	1	4
Rayon/acetate -----------	46	2/	2/
Wool --------------------	19	5	5
	(T-46)	(T-49)	(T-47)
		(Partial tabulations)	

1/ Represents proportion mentioning one or more wool blends, not total of all blends mentioned.
2/ Too few cases to be shown separately.

Use of boys' pants containing combinations of wool and manmade fibers was higher in homes where the family income was $4,000 or over than in homes where the family income was under $4,000. The opposite was true of boys' pants made of wool and cotton mixed. (T-46)

Higher proportions of women living in rural areas than women living in urban or metropolitan areas reported that most of their sons' school pants were "other" cotton. The opposite was true of corduroy and wool pants; those materials were more predominant in metropolitan areas than in smaller cities or rural areas. (T-49)

Fiber preferences for boys' school pants also varied markedly by community size, and, to a lesser extent, by family income, as shown below:

	Mothers who prefer --		
	"Other" cotton	Corduroy	Wool
	Percent	Percent	Percent
Community size:			
Metropolitan ---------	28	46	12
Urban ----------------	54	34	4
Rural ----------------	73	20	1
Family income:			
Under $4,000 ---------	61	27	4
$4,000 to $5,999 -----	57	32	4
$6,000 or over -------	50	34	6
		(T-47)	

Virtually all of those who preferred "other" cotton or corduroy for boys' winter school pants had used their preferred material at some time. (T-46) However, those who named corduroy as the material liked best were much less likely to be using it extensively than were those who liked "other" cotton best. "Other" cotton's popularity for year-round use may partially explain this finding. (T-49)

Reasons for fiber preference

About 9 out of every 10 mothers who mentioned "other" cotton as their preferred fiber for boys' winter school pants said they like it for its good laundering properties. Typical comments made with reference to laundering were: "Cotton pants are easy to wash," "they're washable and don't require special handling." Half of these mothers referred to the good wearing qualities of cotton; about 1 in 3 said they like its appearance, and about 1 in 5 mentioned its warmth and other comfort characteristics. (T-48)

Although corduroy also rated high on laundering characteristics, such as washability and requiring little or no ironing, the outstanding single reason for liking corduroy pants for school during the winter was warmth, mentioned by 66 percent of mothers. Women who said they prefer corduroy also mentioned its good wearing qualities (44 percent), and its good appearance and style (40 percent). (T-48)

Numbers preferring other materials were too small for separate analysis.

Fiber preference in boys' school pants for warmer weather

Virtually all mothers (87 percent) expressed a preference for "other" cotton school pants for warmer weather. Only 3 percent preferred corduroy. Rayon/acetate, rayon-cotton, and Dacron-cotton pants were each preferred by 2 percent of mothers.

Among mothers who preferred cotton --

> 80 percent liked its care and laundering characteristics
> (easy to wash, washes well, etc.)

> 42 percent liked its comfort characteristics
> (cool, absorbent, light weight)

> 33 percent liked its appearance (fresh looking, neater)

> 28 percent liked its durability
> (wears well, lasts a long time)

Ratings of four boys' pants fabrics on selected characteristics

Cotton's strong competitive position in the boys' pants market is documented at another point in the study.

In addition to giving reasons for their fabric preferences in boys' pants, mothers were asked to rate corduroy, "other" cotton, wool blends, and rayon/acetate as very good, good, fair, poor, or very poor on the following characteristics:

> Ease of care (at home -- as distinguished from commercial laundering or dry cleaning)
>
> Durability or wearing qualities
>
> Appearance after washing or cleaning
>
> Not wrinkling

Tables 51 - 54 in the Supplement present detailed results of these ratings, shown by (a) experience with, and (b) preference for the material being rated, where the number of cases involved is sufficient to permit this cross-break. Mothers who expressed no opinion are excluded from these tables. The accompanying chart (fig. 1) shows graphically the proportions who rated each of the four materials as "very good" or "good" on the specified characteristics.

Ratings of "other" cotton pants.--On three factors, namely ease of care, durability, and appearance, "other" cotton received the most favorable ratings of the four fabrics studied. On a fourth factor -- resistance to wrinkling -- cotton, along with wool blends, placed second to corduroy.

Ratings of corduroy pants.--Corduroy received the most favorable vote on resistance to wrinkling. It was runner-up to "other" cotton on ease of care and durability, and tied with wool blends for second place on appearance.

Ratings of wool blends.--Boys' pants made of wool blends scored relatively well on durability, appearance, and resistance to wrinkling, but stood in last place on ease of care (at home).

Ratings of rayon/acetate pants.--Rayon/acetate pants received the least favorable ratings of the fabrics studied on three characteristics -- durability, appearance, and resistance to wrinkling -- and scored almost as low as wool blends on ease of care. (Fig. 1.)

RAISALS OE SELECTED MATERIALS
BOYS' SCHOOL PANTS

Proportion Rating Material as "Very Good"
or "Good" on Each Characteristic

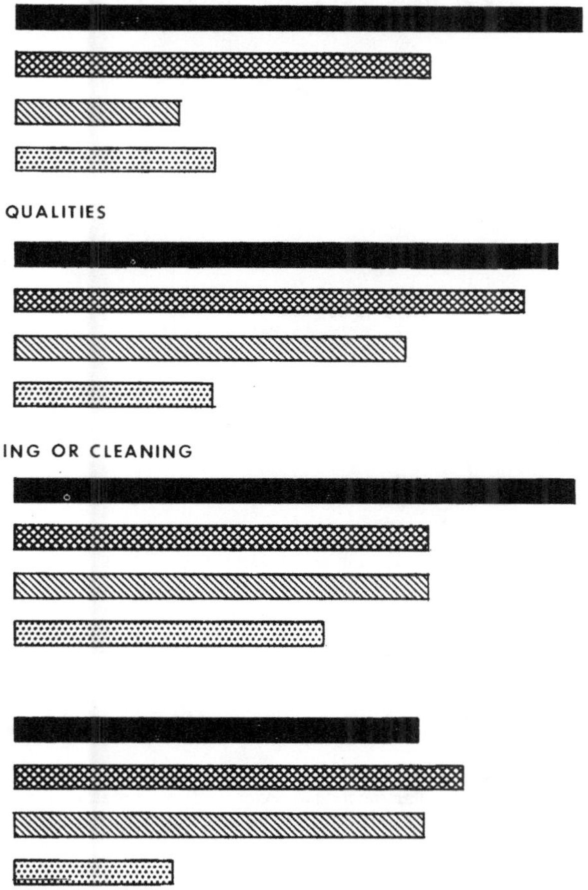

QUALITIES

ING OR CLEANING

Figure 1

Care of boys' school pants

Most boys' school pants are washed rather than dry cleaned. More than 8 out of 10 mothers machine-washed their sons' school pants; 9 percent washed them by hand, and 6 percent had them dry cleaned. (T-50)

Suggestions for improvements

Mothers of school-age boys were asked "Are there any changes or improvements that you would like to see made in boys' school pants?" Close to half (44 percent) made suggestions. Most of the comments were concerned with construction features; the major specific suggestion involved reinforcement of the knees and seat. (T-55)

Rainwear for Boys 6 to 13 years

Ownership

About 6 out of 10 women said their sons owned a regular raincoat. Ownership of boys' rainwear was found to be greater in urban and metropolitan areas than in rural areas. Also, higher proportions of women with family incomes of $4,000 or over reported use of this item than women with family incomes under $4,000.

"Does your boy (do your boys) have a regular raincoat -- the kind that is meant to be worn only in rainy weather?"

	Yes, has raincoat
	Percent
All mothers of boys 6 to 13 --------	57
Community size:	
Metropolitan ---------------------	75
Urban ----------------------------	63
Rural ----------------------------	43
Family income:	
Under $4,000 ---------------------	40
$4,000 to $5,999 ----------------	64
$6,000 or over -------------------	68
	(T-56)

Fiber experience and preference

Rubber-coated cotton was the leading material currently in use for boys' raincoats, with plastic and oilskin tied for second. Forty-five percent of the women reported their boys had rubber-coated cotton, 24 percent plastic, 24 percent oilskin, and 7 percent treated cotton rainwear. (T-57)

Relatively few mothers had had experience with boys' raincoat materials
ther than those in use at present. Half (51 percent) indicated that their
ons had owned rubber-coated cotton coats at some time, 35 percent had experi-
nce with plastic, 30 percent with oilskin, and 11 percent with treated cotton.
T-58)

Rubber-coated cotton was also the material liked best for boys' rainwear;
7 percent preferred it, 21 percent preferred oilskin, and 16 percent plastic.
he majority of the mothers were using their preference at the time of the in-
erview. (T-57,59)

easons for fiber preference

Rubber-coated cotton and oilskin were favored for boys' rainwear primarily
ecause of their water-repellent and durability qualities. Mothers who pre-
erred plastic for boys' rainwear cited convenience, economy, and comfort fac-
ors most often. Typical comments: "Plastic coats are light and easy to fold,
nd carry," "they're waterproof," "they're not very expensive." (T-60)

on-owners of boys' raincoats

In many families, boys wore outer jackets in rainy weather in lieu of
egular raincoats.

Women who said their sons did not own a regular raincoat (43 percent of all
others of boys 6 to 13) were asked what kind of coat their boys wore on rainy
lays. About 9 out of 10 of these women reported the use of some type of outer
jacket. The types specified most frequently were: Regular outer jackets (63
ercent), water-repellent jackets (13 percent), plastic or leather jackets
(10 percent), and reversible jackets (2 percent). Use of regular knee length
oats for rainy weather was reported by 8 percent of the women.

Asked why their sons didn't have a regular raincoat, women gave these reasons most frequently:

	Percent
Raincoats are too expensive ----------	27
Boys have transportation to school ---	26
They dislike wearing raincoats -------	21
They don't need raincoats ------------	14
Their outer jackets are waterproof ---	8

Among non-owners of boys' raincoats, about 2 out of 5 said their boys had
wned a regular raincoat at one time. The kinds of raincoats previously used by
his group of non-owners, and their fabric preferences, are shown below:

	Have used	Like best
	Percent	Percent
Rubber-coated cotton ----	50	36
Plastic -----------------	27	17
Oilskin -----------------	21	22
Treated cotton ----------	8	21

MOTHERS' ATTITUDES TOWARD FIBERS IN SCHOOLGIRLS' CLOTHING

This section deals mainly with mothers' use and opinions of fibers and fiber mixtures in selected items of apparel worn by girls 6 to 13 years of age. The five garments included in the study were blouses, dress-up dresses, slips, skirts, and raincoats. All the schoolgirls' mothers interviewed reported experience with slips; all but 3 percent indicated their daughters wore school blouses, skirts, and dress-up dresses; 6 in 10 said their daughters wore raincoats.

Blouses for School

Fiber experience and preference

Cotton continued to be the dominant fiber in girls' readymade school blouses. Cotton was the most widely used and it was the fiber most mothers liked best for their daughters' school blouses. Cotton blouses were the ones usually worn by 83 percent of the girls in this age category, more than five times as many as usually wore one of the next three most popular fabrics. And cotton was preferred over these three other fabrics combined (nylon, Dacron, and Dacron-cotton) by a margin of 7 to 2. Blouses made of nylon had been tried by half of the mothers, but only 7 percent were using it extensively, or preferred it.

Mothers' Reported Use of and Preference
for Selected Fibers in Girls' School Blouses

	Have used	Most blouses now worn are	Like best
	Percent	Percent	Percent
Cotton -----------------	92	83	71
Nylon -----------------	51	7)	7)
Dacron ----------------	16	4) 15	6) 20
Dacron-cotton ---------	13	4)	7)
	(T-77)	(T-76)	(T-73)

(Partial tabulations)

All but a few of the mothers (98 percent) who preferred cotton for this end-use reported that it dominated their daughters' current blouse wardrobe. Those who liked nylon or Dacron-cotton best were using them to a lesser extent; 8 in 10 of those who preferred nylon had experience with it for girls' blouses, and about 6 in 10 were using it the most "now"; 6 in 10 of those who preferred Dacron-cotton had tried girls' school blouses made of it, and 4 in 10 were using it extensively. (T-76,77)

s preferred cotton for school blouses primarily because they felt
on blouse was easy to launder, and always looked nice. Also, a
others who preferred cotton blouses mentioned their good wearing
   (T-74)

   all mothers who preferred either nylon or a Dacron-cotton blend for
uses mentioned the good laundering characteristics of these two
principally the idea that these blouse materials require little or
. Both nylon and Dacron-cotton were also praised for their appear-
urability characteristics, but to a lesser extent than cotton was
having these two virtues. (T-74)

r preferring Dacron was too small for separate analysis.

tion with preferred fiber

riticisms were made of nylon blouses and Dacron-cotton blouses than
f all-cotton. Nylon blouses were criticized by 37 percent of the
aid they preferred it; Dacron-cotton by 33 percent of its advocates;
ton by 18 percent of its advocates. The chief complaints about
es were that they fray and ravel at the seams, stitching doesn't
turn grey, yellow and dingy, and that they are hard to iron. The
ack of a Dacron-cotton blouse, according to these women, is its
   turn yellow and dingy or to get pilly or fuzzy after washing. The
sk, along with wrinkling, was considered the main disadvantage of all-
uses. (T-75)

Dress-up Dresses

rience and preference

n was the leader in ready-made dress-up dresses for girls of school
nylon its closest competitor. Other materials used with some fre-
e rayon/acetate and Dacron-cotton.

half of the mothers reported that cotton was the predominant fiber in
hters' dress-up wardrobes, compared with 31 percent for nylon, as
w. However, note that preferences for cotton and nylon were almost
ided.

Mothers' Reported Use of and Preference for
Selected Fibers in Girls' Ready-made Dress-up Dresses

	Have used	Most dresses now worn are	Like best
	Percent	Percent	Percent
tton -------------------	82	56	38
lon --------------------	59	31	33
yon/acetate -----------	22	7	5
cron-cotton -----------	11	5	5
	(T-82)	(T-81)	(T-78)
		(Partial tabulations)	

- 19 -

Among those who prefer cotton, more than 9 in 10 said it was the predominant fiber in the dress-up dresses their daughters owned "at present." Of the mothers who preferred nylon, 8 in 10 had used it for girls' dress-up dresses at some time, and 7 in 10 were currently using it extensively. (T-81,82)

Reasons for fiber preference

The dominant factor in the reasons mothers give for preferring cotton for dress-up dresses is appearance and style. Good laundering characteristics and durability were also mentioned frequently. (T-79)

The two chief virtues of nylon for girls' dress-up dresses, according to mothers who preferred this fiber, are ease of care and appearance. Mothers praised nylon because, they say, it requires little or no ironing, it is easy to wash, and it always looks neat and suitable. (T-79)

Numbers preferring other materials were too small for separate analysis.

Dissatisfaction with preferred fiber

Among those who preferred cotton for dress-up dresses, criticisms were very few; only 16 percent mentioned something unfavorable about an all-cotton dress. Criticisms centered around ironing problems and appearance. (T-80)

More than 4 out of 10 mothers who preferred nylon dresses for their daughters had something unfavorable to say about this fiber. Their principal complaints were that nylon is subject to fraying and raveling and that it is too hot. (T-80)

Sources and school use of dress-up dresses

The survey data indicate that in 3 out of 5 homes, girls' dress-up dresses are usually bought new, worn first for parties or other special occasions, and then used for everyday school wear.

Among women who have daughters 6 to 13:

> 63 percent said most of their girls' dress-up dresses
>   were bought new
> 17 percent said most were home-sewn
> 15 percent said most were hand-downs
> 8 percent said most were new gifts

Hand-me-downs (28 percent) and gifts (24 percent) were of greater importance as alternate methods of selecting dress-up dresses, rather than as the main source. (T-69)

Asked whether or not their daughters' dress-up dresses were used for everyday school wear after they become unsuitable for dressy occasions,

> 61 percent said yes, they are used for school
> 33 percent said no, not used for school
> 6 percent gave qualified answers (T-83)

Girls' Slips

Fiber experience and preference

Cotton was the leading fiber for girls' slips, with nylon second. Nine women out of 10 indicated that their school-age daughters had worn cotton slips, while 7 out of 10 reported the use of nylon slips. (T-88)

In terms of preference and predominance in the wardrobe, as the tabulation below shows, cotton had a 2 to 1 lead over nylon, and far outdistanced all other slip materials used. Use of and preference for nylon slips for girls in this age group were greater in homes where the family income was $4,000 or over than in homes where the family income was under $4,000.

Mothers' Reported Use of and Preference
for Selected Fibers in Girls' Slips

	Have used	Most slips now worn are	Like best
	Percent	Percent	Percent
Cotton -------------------	91	66	62
Nylon --------------------	71	31	28
Rayon/acetate ------------	17	3	2
Dacron -------------------	4	1	2
Dacron-cotton ------------	2	1	2
	(T-88)	(T-87)	(T-84)
		(Partial tabulations)	

Reasons for preference and dissatisfaction with preferred fiber

A comparison of the favorable and unfavorable comments volunteered for cotton slips with those volunteered for nylon slips reveals the strong and weak points of each of these materials, as viewed by mothers. Girls' slips made of cotton were thought to be more durable and more comfortable (cooler, not scratchy, etc.) than nylon. Furthermore, women believed that cotton was less likely to turn yellow or dingy after use than nylon. On the other hand, nylon's chief asset was thought to be its ease of care characteristics: Requiring little or no ironing, being easy to launder, and drying quickly. (T-85)

Numbers preferring other materials were too small for separate analysis.

- 21 -

Seasonal use of girls' slips

There appears to be relatively little seasonal variation in the use of slips by girls in the 6 to 13 age range. Large majorities of women reported that their daughters wore either cotton or nylon slips the year round.

"Does your girl (do your girls) wear (cotton) (nylon) slips
the year round or just during certain seasons?"

	Cotton	Nylon
	Percent	Percent
Have used slips of this material --	91	71
Wear year round ------------------	80	58
Just certain seasons ------------	9	9
Not ascertained -----------------	2	4

Of those who did report seasonal use, most said their daughters didn't wear slips during the summer. This was true for cotton as well as nylon users. For the most part, these women felt that any slip would be too warm for their daughters to wear in the summer.

Girls' School Skirts

Sources

Half of the mothers of girls 6 to 13 reported that most of their daughters' school skirts were bought new. One in 5 women indicated that they had made most of their girls' school skirts, and about the same proportion reported hand-me-downs as the major source of skirts for school. (T-70)

Fiber experience and preference for winter

The survey data indicate that many mothers had tried a wide variety of materials for their daughters' skirts. The materials reported most frequently were "other" cotton, all-wool, corduroy, and rayon/acetate. Cotton was the predominant fiber in the school skirts currently owned by half of the girls, wool predominated in 24 percent of the cases, and corduroy in 21 percent.

Most women preferred winter school skirts of natural fibers for their daughters. The three fabrics women liked best were corduroy (25 percent), "other" cotton (16 percent), and all-wool (26 percent). Wool mixtures, such as Dacron-wool, nylon-wool, and Orlon-wool, received a combined preference vote of 14 percent. Corduroy and "other" cotton school skirts were found to be more popular with women living in rural areas than with women living in metropolitan areas, while the reverse was true of all-wool skirts.

Fibers in Girls' School Skirts

	Have used	Most skirts now worn are	Like best
	Percent	Percent	Percent
' cotton -----------	90	50	16
-------------------	74	24	26
y ----------------	55	21	25
acetate -----------	37	1/	1/
-wool -------------	12	5	7
	(T-89)	(T-92)	(T-90)

(Partial tabulations)

oo few cases to be shown separately.

the mothers who liked wool, corduroy, or "other" cotton best
preferred fiber for girls' skirts at some time; three-fourths of
erred Dacron-wool had experience with the mixture in this end-use.

of the fabrics in most of the school skirts in girls' wardrobes,
much more variation. Only among mothers who liked "other"
r winter wear did a substantial majority (more than 9 in 10) re-
use of their preference. About 6 out of 10 of those favoring
y and 4 out of 10 of those favoring Dacron-wool said their pref-
dominant material currently in use for their daughters' school
n's adaptability for several-season use may be an influencing fac-

ber preference

skirts were praised mainly for their warmth, launderability,
ies, and appearance. Except for warmth, the same pattern of
ents was made about "other" cotton skirts for school wear during
T-91)

in appeal for winter school skirts is its warmth, mentioned by
the women who preferred it. Wool also received considerable
appearance -- women said wool skirts don't soil easily, they
ce, and hold their shape. (T-91)

irts made of Dacron-wool appealed to women mainly because they
warm, and make a good appearance, keeping creases or pleats well,
sily, and holding their shape. (T-91)

Fiber preference in school skirts for warmer weather

Cotton was by far the preferred fiber for school skirts during the warm weather. Seventy-eight percent of the women liked cotton best. No other fabric was favored by more than 2 percent of the women interviewed.

Among women who preferred cotton skirts for school during warm weather:

> 70 percent liked its care and laundering characteristics
> (easy to wash, washes well, easy to iron, etc.)
> 49 percent liked its comfort characteristics (cool, absorbent)
> 41 percent liked its appearance (looks nice after use, can be starched)
> 11 percent liked its durability (wears well, holds up under washing)

Ratings of three skirt fabrics on selected characteristics

With the aid of a five-point rating scale ranging from "very good" to "very poor," women were asked to rate each of three skirt materials -- all-cotton, all-wool, and rayon/acetate -- on the following characteristics:

> Ease of care (at home)
> Not wrinkling
> Durability of wearing qualities
> Appearance after washing or cleaning

(Detailed results of these ratings appear in supplemental tables 94, 95, 96.)

Rating of all-cotton skirts.--Virtually all women gave cotton skirts a "good" or "very good" rating on ease of care, durability, and appearance after washing; on a fourth characteristic, resistance to wrinkling, only 1 out of 2 women gave cotton a better than average rating.

Ratings of all-wool skirts.--Wool received its most favorable ratings on durability, appearance after cleaning, and resistance to wrinkling, but showed up rather poorly on ease of care (at home).

Ratings of rayon/acetate skirts.--Rayon/acetate skirts received the least favorable ratings of the three fabrics on resistance to wrinkling, durability, and appearance after cleaning, and did only a little better than wool on ease of care (at home). (Fig. 2.)

MOTHERS' APPRAISALS OE SELECTED MATERIALS FOR GIRLS' SCHOOL SKIRTS

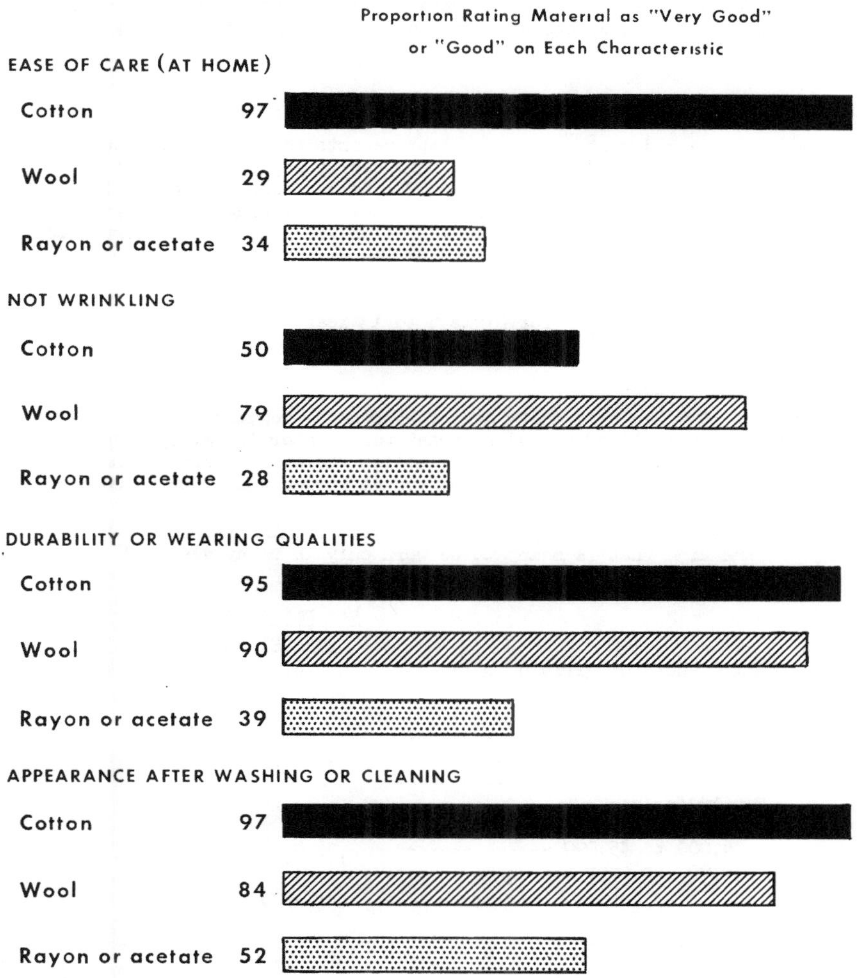

Proportion Rating Material as "Very Good"
or "Good" on Each Characteristic

EASE OF CARE (AT HOME)

Cotton	97
Wool	29
Rayon or acetate	34

NOT WRINKLING

Cotton	50
Wool	79
Rayon or acetate	28

DURABILITY OR WEARING QUALITIES

Cotton	95
Wool	90
Rayon or acetate	39

APPEARANCE AFTER WASHING OR CLEANING

Cotton	97
Wool	84
Rayon or acetate	52

Figure 2

Care of girls' school skirts

Most school skirts are washed, more often in a machine (45 percent) than by hand (28 percent), but 17 percent of the mothers say they usually have skirts dry cleaned. Women reporting extensive use of cotton tended to machine-wash them; about half of those who indicated wool was the dominant fiber in their daughters' skirt wardrobes usually had these skirts dry cleaned, hand washing being favored by another 1 in 3. (T-93)

Suggestions for improving school skirts

Mothers were asked what changes or improvements they would like to see made in school skirts. Three-fourths of them had no suggestions to offer. Those who did talked mainly about the need for better constructed skirts, and ones that would be washable and require a minimum of ironing. In addition, a number of women suggested that a better selection (more colors, patterns and styles, etc.) be made available.

Rainwear for Girls 6 to 13 Years

Ownership

Six out of 10 women said their daughters owned a regular raincoat. Like boys' rainwear, ownership of girls' rainwear was greater in metropolitan and urban areas than in rural areas, and in families where the annual income was $4,000 or over than in families where the annual income was under $4,000.

"Does your girl (do your girls) have a regular raincoat -- the kind that is meant to be worn only in rainy weather?"

	Yes, has raincoat Percent
All mothers of girls 6 to 13 ----	60
Community size:	
Metropolitan ------------------	72
Urban -------------------------	69
Rural -------------------------	45
Family income:	
Under $4,000 ------------------	48
$4,000 to $5,999 --------------	63
$6,000 or over ----------------	70
	(T-97)

Fiber experience and preference

Plastic was the leading material currently in use for girls' raincoats, with rubber-coated cotton second, and treated cotton third. Forty-four percent of the women indicated their daughters owned a plastic raincoat, 26 percent

ed cotton, 18 percent treated cotton, 7 percent oilskin, and
A majority of the mothers had not tried any girls' raincoat
in that in use at the time of the interview. (T-98, 99)

ressed fiber preferences were about evenly divided among the
at materials -- plastic (25 percent), treated cotton (24 per-
-coated cotton (22 percent). The majority of the mothers
preference "at present." (T-99, 100)

preference

l reasons women gave for preferring plastic coats were that
roof, inexpensive, lightweight, easy to fold and carry, and
f. Treated cotton coats were preferred mainly because of
their versatility (suitable for many occasions), and their
teristics. Rubber-coated cotton was liked especially for its
nd durability qualities and its appearance. (T-101)

·ls' raincoats

;irls who did not own a regular raincoat were asked what kinds
ughters wore on rainy days. About half of them reported the
:ets of one type or another, and a few more than a third re-
' regular knee-length coats during rainy weather.

ieir daughters didn't have a regular raincoat, women gave
it frequently:

	Percent
.ncoats are too expensive -----	25
·ls have transportation to	
·hool ------------------------------	25
need for a raincoat ----------	16
·y dislike wearing raincoats --	11
:ir coats or jackets are water-	
·oof ------------------------------	10

mers of girls' raincoats, almost half (47 percent) said their
ι regular raincoat at one time. The kinds of raincoats pre-
.his group of non-owners, and their fabric preferences, are

	Have used	Like best
	Percent	Percent
ιstic ----------------	53	20
·ber-coated cotton ---	19	15
:ated cotton ---------	16	35
·on ------------------	6	2
.skin ----------------	4	4

- 27 -

OPINIONS ABOUT OTHER CLOTHING ITEMS WORN BY CHILDREN 1 TO 13

Two additional items worn by both boys and girls from 1 to 13 years of age -- outer jackets for winter wear and anklets or socks -- were covered by this survey. Mothers were also asked a few questions about children's "wash-and-wear" clothes and about their experience with washing children's woolen garments.

Anklets and Socks

While the questionnaire for this study was being tested, it became apparent that most mothers could speak more easily about their opinions of stretch or regular socks than of the materials from which the socks were made, so the questions were phrased in those terms. Since cotton is the major fiber in regular socks and nylon in stretch socks, the attitudes expressed as an evaluation of the socks in effect often indirectly include an evaluation of the material from which they are made.

Use of stretch socks

Ownership of children's stretch socks was widespread. About 9 out of 10 women reported their children had worn this type of sock. Use of children's stretch socks was reported by somewhat higher proportions of women in families where the annual income was $4,000 or over than in the families where the income was under $4,000. (T-1)

Fiber experience

Three-fifths (61 percent) of the women indicated their children had worn stretch socks made of nylon; about a fourth (23 percent) reported the use of a nylon and cotton mix and one-tenth reported the use of all-cotton stretch socks. (T-1)

When asked what materials their children's regular socks were made of, 92 percent of the women said cotton. Other materials reported were nylon (8 percent), wool (5 percent), and rayon (4 percent). (T-2)

Stretch versus regular socks

Users of children's stretch socks were asked whether they preferred stretch or regular socks for their children. Opinions divided fairly evenly; about half of these women said they preferred stretch socks, and the other half said they preferred regular socks. (T-3)

Reasons for preference

Women who preferred stretch socks for their children gave reasons relating to comfort, fit, and durability most often. Typical comments: "Stretch socks fit smoothly," "you don't need to worry about the size," "they last a long time." To some of these women the fact that they dry quickly was also an advantage.

Mothers who liked regular socks better cited a variety of reasons for their choice without stressing any of them; factors such as not turning grey or dingy, durability, and absorbency were mentioned a little more often than other reasons. (T-4)

Dissatisfaction with stretch or regular socks

About 4 in 10 women who preferred stretch socks for their children mentioned something they didn't like about these socks. The major drawback cited was that they turned yellow or dingy after use.

Thirty-five percent of the women who preferred children's regular socks mentioned something they disliked about them. The leading criticisms were that regular socks don't wear well and have a tendency to stretch at the tops. (T-5)

Interest expressed in stretch socks by non-users

Women who said their children had never worn stretch socks were asked whether or not they would be interested in getting them. Three out of 10 of these women said they would be interested. The remaining 7 in 10 women either said they wouldn't be interested (51 percent) or were undecided (18 percent).

Lack of enthusiasm for children's stretch socks was based primarily on the belief that these socks don't fit well, that they're too hot, and too expensive.

Outer Jackets for Winter

Ownership

To insure that the term "outer jacket" had the same meaning for all respondents, interviewers were instructed to read the following definition before asking any questions:

> I'd like to talk about the outdoor type jackets or
> short coats -- like zipper jackets, car coats, and
> parkas -- that are worn by boys and girls during
> colder weather. We are not interested in snowsuits,
> full-length topcoats, or overcoats.

Use of outer jackets of this type is practically universal. Ninety-seven percent of the mothers of children 1 to 13 said their children had worn this kind of garment for outdoor activities during the preceding year.

Sources

Majorities, ranging from 57 percent of the mothers of pre-school girls to 83 percent of the mothers of schoolboys, indicated that most of their children's outer jackets worn in the past year were bought for them. "Hand-downs" from older brothers or sisters and friends and relatives was the next most frequent source. Relatively few women said they made most of the children's jackets or that most of them were received as gifts.

Most Frequent Sources of Outer Jackets Worn by Children 1 to 13 During the Year Preceding the Interview

	Girls 1 to 5	Boys 1 to 5	Girls 6 to 13	Boys 6 to 13
	Percent	Percent	Percent	Percent
Bought new ---------	57	66	75	83
Handed down --------	27	25	15	13
As new gifts -------	6	5	3	3
Home sewn ----------	4	2	2	--
	(T-26)	(T-15)	(T-71)	(T-38)

Fiber experience

Cotton led a long list of jacket materials with which women claimed experience. Use of cotton jackets was reported by 8 in 10 women, wool by almos 6 in 10, and rayon/acetate by about 3 in 10. Other materials mentioned by mo than 10 percent of the women were leather (or suede), nylon, and mixtures of cotton and wool.

Although cotton jackets predominate in children's current wardrobes, mothers express a preference for wool over cotton by a margin of 3 to 2.

Mothers' Reported Use of and Preference for Selected Fibers in Children's Outer Jackets

	Have used	Most jackets now worn are	Like best
	Percent	Percent	Percent
Cotton ------------	80	46	22
Wool --------------	56	28	34
Rayon/acetate ------	32	3	--
Leather or suede ---	17	4	5
Nylon -------------	16	6	7
Cotton-wool --------	14	7	8
Nylon-wool ---------	4	2	4
Dacron-wool -------	4	2	3
	(T-102)	(T-105)	(T-103)
		(Partial tabulations)	

Virtually all (99 percent) of those women preferring cotton had tried it for outer jackets at some time. Almost 9 out of 10 who like wool or leather best had experience with these materials in jackets. Among those favoring cotton-wool, nylon, nylon-wool, and Dacron-wool, from 56 to 72 percent were familiar with their preference in this type of garment. (T-102)

9 in 10 of those who preferred cotton reported that most of the
:heir children were wearing that winter were made of this fiber.
lked the other materials best, proportions ranging from 43 to 64
:ed their sons and daughters were currently wearing the preferred
-105)

)er preference

:d many things they liked about the material they preferred for
's outer jackets. Jackets or short coats made of all-wool, wool
:ather were highly praised for their warmth, while ones made of
ll-cotton were highly praised for their ease of care qualities.
: the principal comments given for seven outer jacket materials:

:red mainly for its warmth (92 percent), but also for good ap-
  (38 percent) and durability (29 percent).

:d for its ease of care (36 percent), washability (32 percent),
.31 percent), appearance (30 percent) and durability (26 percent).

: its warmth (69 percent) and laundering qualities (40 percent).

 of care (59 percent), washability (39 percent), warmth
:ent) and appearance (35 percent).

:mth (60 percent), wind resistance (41 percent), durability
:rcent), the fact that they can be sponged off (38 percent),
)pearance (37 percent).

 warmth (70 percent), good laundering properties (53 percent)
l appearance (41 percent).

: warmth (65 percent), laundering characteristics (54 percent)
id appearance (41 percent).

                        (T-104)

:e outer jacket materials on selected characteristics

10 said their children had worn outer jackets were asked to rate,
? the five-point scale, each of three outer jacket fibers --
ind rayon/acetate -- on these characteristics:

                Ease of care (at home)
                Not showing dirt
                Durability or wearing qualities
                Appearance after washing or
                  cleaning

'Detailed results of these ratings appear in Supplement
  tables 107, 108, and 109.)

MOTHERS' APPRAISALS OF SELECTED MATERIALS FOR CHILDREN'S OUTER JACKETS

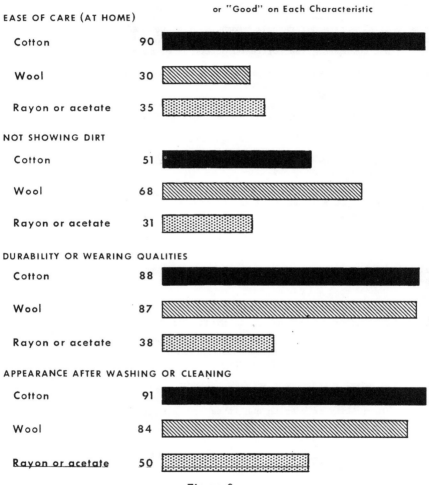

Proportion Rating Material as 'Very Good" or "Good" on Each Characteristic

EASE OF CARE (AT HOME)

Cotton 90

Wool 30

Rayon or acetate 35

NOT SHOWING DIRT

Cotton 51

Wool 68

Rayon or acetate 31

DURABILITY OR WEARING QUALITIES

Cotton 88

Wool 87

Rayon or acetate 38

APPEARANCE AFTER WASHING OR CLEANING

Cotton 91

Wool 84

Rayon or acetate 50

Figure 3

Ratings of cotton jackets.--Among the three outer-jacket fabrics appraised, cotton had by far the best reputation on ease of care at home. Ninety percent of the women rated cotton "very good" or "good" on this characteristic. It scored about as high on durability and on appearance, although not by as wide a margin, and ranked second to wool on not showing dirt.

Ratings of wool jackets.--Wool scored very well on durability and appearance, although a little behind cotton on these factors. It ranked highest of the three fibers on not showing dirt, but made a relatively poor showing on ease of care at home.

Ratings of rayon/acetate jackets.--Overall, rayon received the least praise of the three fibers under consideration. It was outdistanced by both cotton and wool on not showing dirt, durability and appearance, and barely nudged wool out for second place on ease of care at home. (Fig. 3.)

Care of children's outer jackets

The survey data indicate that almost as many women washed their children's outer jackets as sent them out to be dry cleaned. Forty-three percent said they usually machine or hand washed their children's jackets while 47 percent said they usually had them dry cleaned.

Whether an outer jacket was usually washed or dry cleaned naturally depended to a large extent on its fiber content. Jackets made of all-wool or a wool and cotton mix were usually dry cleaned, while cotton or nylon jackets were usually washed. In the case of rayon and leather, almost as many women took care of them at home as had them dry cleaned. (T-106)

Suggestions for improving children's outer jackets

Seven out of 10 women offered no suggestions as to how children's outer jackets or short coats might be improved. The principal suggestions offered by those who mentioned ideas were:

	Percent
Improve the zippers in outer jackets --	5
Provide a better selection, more color, styles, etc. ------------------	5
Make children's jackets more protective -----------------------------	4
Make more jackets that are washable ---	4
Reinforce the elbows ------------------	4
Make allowances for growth ------------	2
Improve jacket linings ----------------	2
Do away with zippers ------------------	2

Washing Woolen Items

A little over half (54 percent) of the mothers interviewed indicated they had washed some woolen children's clothing items in the past year or so, mainly sweaters. Other wool items washed were skirts, socks, slacks, outer jackets, sport shirts, gloves, hats, and scarves. (T-119, 120)

Mothers who had washed woolen items divided almost evenly when asked about the tags the garments carried; a few more than a third said the wool garments they washed were labeled washable, about one-third said they were not labeled, and the remaining third couldn't recall anything about the labeling. Only 1 in 5 who had washed wool expressed dissatisfaction with the results. Shrinkage was the major complaint; matting, loss of shape and fading were also mentioned.

A few women (one-tenth of those dissatisfied) confessed they had put woolen things in washing machines and therefore felt that they themselves were responsible for the unsatisfactory results.

Children's "Wash-and-Wear" Clothing

In the development phase of the study, it became evident that the term "wash-and-wear" meant different things to different women. In order to insure that all respondents had the same concept of "wash-and-wear," interviewers were instructed to read the following definition before they asked any questions on this subject:

> As you know, there are clothes nowadays that are
> called "drip-dry" or "wash-and-wear." These are
> usually advertised as washable and neat enough to
> wear with little or no ironing. I'm not talking
> about children's clothes like corduroy, denim, or
> seersucker, that are seldom ironed anyway.

Use of "wash-and-wear"

Three-fourths of the mothers report that their children have worn "wash-and-wear" garments. There is no marked variation among mothers of different ages or between urban and rural dwellers, but a somewhat higher proportion of mothers in families with higher incomes report the use of "wash-and-wear" clothing than is the case among mothers in the $4,000 and under income bracket. (T-111)

"Wash-and-wear" clothing is more widely used by girls than by boys. About four-fifths (78 percent) of mothers of girls, compared with three-fifths (59 percent) of mothers of boys, report the use of these garments.

Dresses are the "wash-and-wear" items most likely to be worn by girls; shirts are the leading "wash-and-wear" items worn by boys. Dresses are mentioned by 65 percent of the mothers of girls, blouses by 53 percent, and skirts by 31 percent. Shirts are mentioned by 53 percent of mothers of boys, and trousers by 24 percent. (T-112, 113)

Satisfaction with children's "wash-and-wear" garments

Satisfaction with children's "wash-and-wear" garments is at a fairly high level. Among users, favorable comments about "wash-and-wear" outnumber unfavorable comments by a wide margin; over half (62 percent) indicated there wasn't anything they didn't like so well about this type of clothing for children. (T-114, 115)

Ease of care, particularly as it relates to ironing, is the major appeal "wash-and-wear" has for mothers.

"What things do you like best about children's 'wash-and-wear' clothes?"

	Mothers of children who have worn "wash-and-wear"
	Percent
Ease of care ---------------	87
Require little or no ironing -----------------	56
Easy to wash -------------	23
Dry quickly --------------	12
Easy to iron ------------	10
Appearance and style -------	23

(T-114)

(Partial tabulation)

Further evidence of the ease of care appeal of "wash-and-wear" for children is found in the responses these mothers give to the direct question, "All in all, would you say that children's 'wash-and-wear' clothes are a lot easier, a little easier, or not as easy to take care of as other clothes?"

66 percent say that "wash-and-wear" is a lot easier to take care of
24 percent say a little easier
5 percent say not as easy
3 percent say about the same
2 percent express no opinion

- 35 -

Dissatisfaction with children's "wash-and-wear"

Any lack of enthusiasm for "wash-and-wear" stems primarily from the belief that these clothes do require some ironing.

When users were asked to mention anything about children's "wash-and-wear" that they didn't like, the most frequent complaint, mentioned by about one woman out of five, is that "wash-and-wear" garments have to be ironed.

Fiber experience

Use of children's "wash-and-wear" made from manmade fibers such as nylon, Dacron, or Orlon, is reported by 70 percent of the women who say their children have worn "wash-and-wear." Mixtures of cotton and manmade fibers have been tried by 59 percent and all-cotton by 55 percent. (T-116)

(NOTE: Any figures based on respondents' recall of fiber experience are subject to errors of memory or misinformation. In the case of "wash-and-wear" clothing, another source of error is the tendency of some respondents to assume that "wash-and-wear" items must contain some manmade fiber or be entirely made from a manmade fiber.)

Fiber preference

Among women who have used children's "wash-and-wear," about 4 in 10 express no particular fiber preference. Twenty-eight percent indicate a preference for cotton, 16 percent for cotton and manmade mixtures, and 17 percent for all-manmade. Preference for manmade fibers is highest among women living in the metropolitan cities, while preference for all-cotton is highest among women living in rural and urban areas. (T-117)

Manmade fibers seem to rate better than all-cotton in one respect: Requiring little or no ironing is mentioned far less often as a reason for preferring cotton "wash-and-wear" than for preferring the other two types. On two factors, durability and coolness, cotton receives a higher proportion of mentions than manmade or a mixture of cotton and manmade fibers.